BRAVE BEAR

AND THE GHOSTS

A SIOUX LEGEND

ADAPTED AND RETOLD BY
GLORIA DOMINIC

ILLUSTRATED BY
CHARLES REASONER

One night long ago in the land of ghosts, where it is always winter, a ghost called out into the darkness for his friends. Before long three ghosts joined him. The four friends talked of ghostly things. As they did, they laughed about their many adventures.

Soon the conversation turned to the many pranks the four had played upon the living. The ghosts tried to outdo one another with wild descriptions of their exploits.

"I have tricked so many people, it's impossible to count them all," boasted one.

"You haven't tricked as many as I have," said another. "The humans I have haunted were scared out of their wits."

The third ghost said, "I find it very easy to scare people. They are all frightened of ghosts, aren't they?"

"Not so," said the fourth ghost in a mysterious voice.

"What do you mean?" the others asked.

"I have heard of a young man called Brave Bear. It is said he is afraid of nothing," replied the fourth ghost. "Brave Bear is a warrior and a hunter who laughs in the face of death. The people say his strength and courage can conquer any foe. In games of speed or cunning, he is said to have no equal."

"Hah," said the second ghost. "I do not believe it."

"Neither do I," said the third. "I'm sure I could scare this man."

"Let us make a bet to see who can scare this young man," suggested the first ghost, who was always looking for some sport. "Each of us has a very fine ghost horse. The one who succeeds in scaring Brave Bear wins all of the horses."

"Agreed," said the others.

It was not long before the ghosts had their chance. The very next night, a full moon shone. It peeked between the trees of the forest, casting long shadows upon the path.

Most people did not like to go out walking at night, for none were eager to meet a ghost. But true to his reputation, Brave Bear was not afraid of the night—or of running into a ghost. "Ghosts were once alive, the way I am now," he would say. "Someday, I, too, will be dead. So, in truth, we are really all the same!"

The night of the full moon, Brave Bear walked among the shadows, enjoying the quiet forest. As he walked, he hummed a song. He liked the way it echoed softly among the trees.

Suddenly, a shape appeared in front of him!

"Aieee!" said the first ghost, jumping out from behind a tree. He waved his long skeleton bones in the face of the man. His skeleton horse reared and whinnied eerily.

Instead of fleeing, Brave Bear calmly looked at the skeleton.

"Good evening, friend," said the young man. "Are you cold? You are shaking very hard. Indeed, it must be cold without skin and blood to warm you."

"I am a ghost!" screamed the skeleton. "I do not feel the cold! I am here to haunt you."

"Well, you can try," said Brave Bear. "But please do not take up too much time. I am enjoying the night air and would like to be on my way."

The ghost grew angry at this unexpected answer. "We will see how tough you are," he hissed. "Let us shoot arrows at this tree. I know I can beat you. When I do, I will turn you into a ghost."

"Very well," agreed Brave Bear. "But let us make a wager. If you win, you may do as you say. If I win, I will take your horse."

Before the ghost could say a word, Brave Bear seized him and broke off a long leg bone with a *snap!* Then, with amazing speed, the young man bent the bone into a bow shape and strung it. He quickly pulled off both arm bones of the skeleton. "I think these will work quite well as arrows," he said.

The young man took his new bow and arrows. He aimed at the tree and hit it squarely. "Your turn," said Brave Bear to the ghost.

The ghost sat in a broken heap upon the ground. "Aieee!" he cried. "Look what you've done to me. How can I take aim without my leg or arms?"

"I see what you mean," said Brave Bear. "I guess this means I win our little bet." He led the ghost horse away, humming the song he liked so well.

"I'll get you for this!" the ghost shouted after him. But Brave Bear was not afraid.

13

Brave Bear walked along. It wasn't long before he heard an unusual moaning in the trees. "Hooooo-heeeee! Hooooo-heeeee!" Others might have been afraid of the noise, but not Brave Bear. In fact, he did not seem the least bit surprised when the second ghost galloped up to him on another skeleton horse.

"Hooooo-heeeee! Hoka-hey!" the ghost cried. "It is a good day to die!"

"Very well," replied Brave Bear. "But to make things interesting, let's make a bet. I can tell that you have a very fine singing voice. I also enjoy singing and making music. Let us see who can make the best music. If you win, you can do whatever you like with me. If I win, I will take your horse."

Before the second ghost could argue, Brave Bear cracked the neck of his foe. Then he took off the ghost's hand, with its long-boned fingers. Setting the ghost's skull on the ground, the young man grabbed a stout stick. *Rat-a-tat. Rat-a-tat.* Brave Bear beat the stick upon the skull in a steady rhythm, singing loudly all the time. With his other hand, he rattled the skeleton's hand, *clack-a-clack, clack-a-clack.*

"Ouch!" cried the ghost.

"Is that the best song you can sing?" asked Brave Bear. "You have lost our bet." He hurled the screaming skull up into a tree, where it landed in a crow's nest. Then Brave Bear led away the two ghost horses.

Before long, the third ghost jumped out from behind a tree. His horse followed behind. "Again?" sighed Brave Bear. "I never knew the forest to be such a crowded place!"

"Beware," said the ghost. "You are in danger."

"In danger of what?" the young man asked, laughing.

"In danger of me!" howled the ghost.

"If you say so," said Brave Bear. "But before you harm me, would you like to make a small bet?"

"What sort of bet?" asked the ghost.

"See that ice over there?" said Brave Bear, pointing to a small pond. "It's the perfect place to spin a top. Let's have a contest to see whose top can spin the longest. If you win, I will gladly give you the charmed bear tooth I wear around my neck. If I succeed, your horse is mine."

"What will we use for tops?" asked the ghost skeleton.

"I don't know about you, but I'm going to use these!" replied Brave Bear. Before the ghost knew what had happened, the young brave reached into the skeleton's mouth and yanked out all his teeth.

Brave Bear drove a small stick into each tooth and ran to the pond. "Watch this," he called, expertly spinning the tops.

The angry ghost rushed over to the pond. He was just about to catch Brave Bear when he slipped on the ice. "Ow!" the toothless skeleton cried as he fell, scattering his bones across the frozen pond.

"You should not have tried to run on the ice," scolded Brave Bear. "Now you have cracked your nice white rib bones. Oh, well, I must be going. Thank you for the horse."

Again, Brave Bear set off, this time leading three horses along the path.

The fourth ghost had been watching the young man from behind a tree. "This Brave Bear really is all they say," the ghost remarked. "But I will surprise him. Then we will see how brave he is."

So the ghost sat upon its skeleton horse, waiting for Brave Bear to pass by. When the young man did, the skeleton let out a bloodcurdling cry and leaped upon Brave Bear's back.

Instead of being frightened, Brave Bear simply said, "Ho, friend. Are you a tired old ghost? You seem to be in need of someone to carry you. Do not worry, you are light. I will help you."

"Put me down," insisted the ghost, who was insulted by this offer.

"All right," said Brave Bear. "But before you go, let's play a game. I love guessing games. Take a small stone and hide it in your hand. If I can guess which hand the stone is in, I win your fine horse. If you can fool me, all four horses are yours!"

The ghost agreed and picked up a stone. Hiding both fists behind its back, the ghost said, "Guess which hand!"

Brave Bear smiled. Because he could see right through the skeleton's ribs, the stone was easy to spot!

"Oh, this is hard," said Brave Bear, frowning and scratching his head. "But I think the stone is in your left hand."

"How did you know?" shouted the ghost, angrily rushing toward Brave Bear.

"Because I am a ghost, too," Brave Bear shouted back in an even louder voice. "And I'm going to get you!"

The frightened ghost turned and ran through the trees. In its haste, it tripped and landed in a half-frozen stream. Brave Bear laughed. "Good for you," he said. "You will be nice and clean after your bath. The girls are sure to like you!"

"How dare you!" said the ghost. "I am a girl."

"Sorry," said Brave Bear. "It's hard to tell." Then he smiled and climbed upon the fourth horse, leading the other horses behind him.

J ust before sunrise, Brave Bear reached the tipis of his people. Some children were out early, playing in the meadow. When they saw Brave Bear and the skeleton horses, they screamed in fright. Running to their tipis, the children awakened the grown-ups to tell them what they had seen.

As the people came out, the sun rose, and Brave Bear saw that it was springtime. The ghost horses faded away in the light.

"I have had an interesting night in the forest," Brave Bear said. He told everyone the story of his adventures with the ghosts.

"You really are afraid of nothing!" said a small girl in wonder.

Brave Bear smiled proudly. Then he felt a funny tickling on his arm. Looking down, he spied a tiny ant crawling on him.

"Aieee!" he cried. "Get it off before it bites me!"

So the little girl gently flicked the ant into the grass, saving Brave Bear from the one little thing he was afraid of.

The Sioux

THE SIOUX

Sioux Homeland

Long ago, the Sioux lived in the woodlands of what is now Minnesota. Men hunted and fished, while women raised crops and gathered wild rice and berries.

By the 1700s, they had settled on the Great Plains in the present-day states of North Dakota, South Dakota, Nebraska and Montana. Partly to flee rival Ojibwas who had acquired guns, they also moved to follow the buffalo herds, which became easier to hunt with the introduction of horses.

Buffalo meant everything to the Plains people. It provided food, clothing, shelter, utensils, and fuel. When the Sioux moved to the plains, herds of up to a hundred million buffalo roamed the land.

They lived in tipis, made of poles and buffalo hide. Tipis were warm in winter, cool in summer, and could withstand strong prairie winds. Most importantly, they could be easily taken down and assembled again for the constantly-moving people.

Life on the Great Plains was not easy. In summer, there were harsh winds and high temperatures. The land was dry and prone to fires, and floods during rain. Winter meant snow and freezing temperatures.

Right. Beaded bags were used to carry tobacco and medicines.

Above. Plains Indians decorated themselves and their clothes with beads and shells as this Sioux girl, Standing Holy Water, has done.

Sioux People

The word "Sioux" came from rival Ojibwas, meaning "snake," a metaphor for enemy. They called themselves Dakota, Lakota, or Nakota, depending on the language dialect they spoke, which meant "allies." They also called themselves the "Seven Council Fires."

Left. A dog pulling a travois, which carried the tribe's belongings across the plains.

Each council fire had separate leadership, but they united for important decisions. The largest council fire was on the Western Plains and was divided into seven Lakota-speaking groups called the Teton Sioux. Two councils on the Middle Plains spoke Nakota and were called the Yankton Sioux. The Santee Sioux lived on the Eastern Plains and spoke Dakota. Together, they were the dominant power on the Great Plains, known for their bravery and honorable actions.

They were nomads—always on the move following buffalo herds. Possessions and people were carried on two poles in an "A" shape with the pointed end attached to a dog or a horse and the other end dragging on the ground. This was called a travois, and it allowed the people to move their belongings easily. The men hunted, took care of the horses, made weapons, waged war and performed religious ceremonies. The women tended camp by tanning hides and making tipis, clothing and furnishings. They gathered and prepared the food, cared for the children and were responsible for moving the camp. Children were expected to do chores as well.

Prayer and religious ceremonies were very important. They had prayers for all aspects of their lives. The buffalo played a meaningful role in the spiritual world, just as it did in the practical world.

Food and Clothing

Everything they needed for a comfortable life came from the buffalo. Food consisted mostly of buffalo meat, fresh, dried and raw; and sometimes deer, elk, and porcupine. Before Europeans introduced metal pots and pans, women used the stomachs of buffaloes to cook. Food, such as stews and mush, was placed in the stomach along with hot rocks, which would bring the contents of the stomach to a boil. Gathered seeds, vegetables, nuts and berries added to the diet. Clothing was usually made of tanned hide. This process of making animal skin into leather took a lot of work and a special chemical mixture of buffalo brains and liver. Hides not only made clothing, but tipis, blankets, robes, parfleches (pouches), shields and moccasins.

Men wore fringed shirts and leggings. On important occasions, chiefs wore long regal headdresses of eagle feathers and fur. Women wore ankle-length fringed dresses and leggings. Both wore elaborately decorated moccasins, gloves, and vests, and jewelry made of feathers, quills, and beads.

Tipis, robes, and shields were painted with pictures telling of important events or brave deeds in colors that had special meanings. Shells, dyed porcupine quills, glass beads and buttons (acquired by trading), and feathers were used for decoration on clothing and leather goods.

Above. Women stretching buffalo hides, held in place with rope of buffalo sinew.
Right. A beautifully beaded tomahawk peacepipe.

Below. Chief Spotted Tail and his wife dressed for a special occasion.

39

Left. Buffalo horn that was used to carry paint, medicine, and herbs.

Sioux Today

The Sioux live with non-natives in many of the major cities in the United States and on reservations in Minnesota, South Dakota, North Dakota, Nebraska, and Montana. Some enjoy careers such as medicine, law and writing, while others work recreating and studying the traditional crafts and ways.

Like other nations, they are experiencing an explosion of interest in the traditional ways. Dancing and singing are still very important. Gatherings called powwows bring different nations together from all over the country to celebrate Native American culture.

Above. Long-tipped lances like this were used in hunting buffalo.

Above. Shields were made of buffalo hide and painted with important images from visions that offered spiritual protection.

Glossary

Akicita: Camp police

Counting coup: A way of winning personal honor in warfare that did not always mean destroying the enemy. You scored a coup when you touched an enemy with a coup stick

Ghost Dance: A ceremony of chants and communal dancing. If the ritual was followed, it promised the return to life of dead ancestors, the end of the white man, and the return of the buffalo and the way of life before the white man arrived

Nomads: People who move from place to place to find food

Parfleche: Decorated pouch made of rawhide to carry small items, dried food, and pemmican

Pemmican: A trail food made of meat, fat and berries

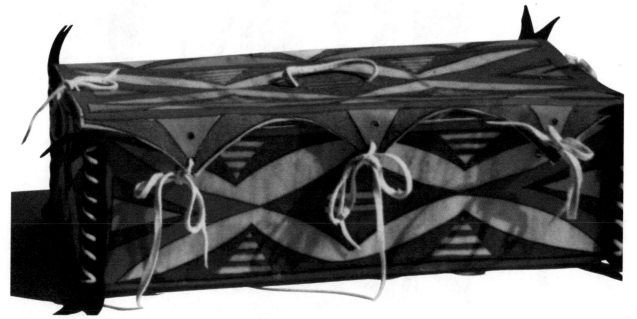

Above. A brightly painted parfleche. Parfleches were traditionally painted by women and were the drawers and closets of Plains Indians.

Left. A bead-covered amulet, in the shape of a bald eagle, held a child's umbilical cord. These good-luck charms were worn around the child's neck or they were attached to the cradleboard.

Below. Modern-day hoop dancers, like this boy, wear beautifully ornamented costumes.

Powwow: A festive gathering that includes dancing, singing and food

Shaman: A spiritual leader trained to heal the sick, interpret signs and dreams, and perform rituals and ceremonies

Sun Dance: The most important ceremony of the year, held to thank the Great Spirit for past blessings and to pray for future ones

Sweat lodge: A rounded house, heated by steam from water poured on hot rocks, where participants, such as warriors and hunters, pray as their bodies are purified through sweating

Travois: A device to carry people and belongings. It consisted of two long poles, one end fastened to a dog or horse, and the other end dragging on the ground

Many plains people used buffalo skulls in religious ceremonies.

Important Dates

1700s: The Sioux become expert horsemen

1803: Louisiana Purchase. United States purchases land from the Mississippi River to the Rocky Mountains from France. The land doubles the size of the United States, eventually becoming parts of the states of Missouri, Arkansas, Louisiana, Minnesota, South Dakota, North Dakota, Nebraska, Kansas, Oklahoma, and Texas.

1867–83: Extermination of over 13 million buffalo by white men

1876: Sioux, Cheyenne and Arapaho win the Battle of Little Bighorn

1890: The Battle of Wounded Knee ends the Indian Wars

1924: All Native Americans born in the U.S. declared citizens

1968: Indian Civil Rights Act gives Native Americans the right to govern themselves on their reservations

1982: The Sioux nation loses a case in the U.S. Supreme Court to regain ownership of the Black Hills of South Dakota

1979: The U.S. Supreme Court awards the Sioux nation $105 million for the taking of their lands, resolving legal action begun in 1923.

PHOTO CREDITS

Pages 32-33: Cliff with trees, Photo by Dave Albers
              Red Cloud, Courtesy of the Siouxland Heritage Museums, Sioux Falls, South Dakota

Pages 34-35: Map and buffalo by Dave Albers
              Tipis, Photo by Dave Albers, Courtesy of a Private Collection

Pages 36-37: Sioux girl, Courtesy of the Siouxland Heritage Museums, Sioux Falls, South Dakota
              Beaded Bags, Photos by Dave Albers, Courtesy of a Private Collection
              Dog and travois by Charles Reasoner

Pages 38-39: Women with hides, and Chief with Wife, Courtesy of the Siouxland Heritage Museums,
              Sioux Falls, South Dakota
              Beaded peacepipe/hatchet, Photo by Dave Albers, Courtesy of a Private Collection

Pages 40-41: Horn, lance, and shield, Photos by Dave Albers, Courtesy of a Private Collection

Pages 42-43: Parfleche and amulet, Photos by Dave Albers, Courtesy of a Private Collection
              Dancer, Courtesy of the Siouxland Heritage Museums, Sioux Falls, South Dakota

Pages 44-45: Skull, Photo by Dave Albers, Courtesy of a Private Collection
              Red Cloud, Courtesy of the Siouxland Heritage Museums, Sioux Falls, South Dakota

Pages 46-48: Chief Spotted Tail and wife, and tipis scene, Courtesy of the Siouxland Heritage Museums,
              Sioux Falls, South Dakota
              War club and beadwork, Photos by Dave Albers, Courtesy of a Private Collection

SIOUX BIBLIOGRAPHY

Bleeker, Sonia. The Sioux Indians. New York: William Morrow & Co., 1962.

Brandon, Alvin M. The American Heritage Book of Indians. New York: American
Heritage Publishing Co., Inc., 1961.

Brooks, Barbara. The Sioux. Vero Beach, FL: Rourke Publications, 1989.

Capps, Benjamin. The Old West: The Indians. New York: Time-Life Books, 1973.

Erdoes, Richard. The Sun Dance People: The Plains Indians, Their Past and Present.
New York: Knopf, 1972.

Landau, Elaine. The Sioux. New York: Franklin Watts, 1989.

Osinski, Alice. The Sioux. Chicago: Children's Press, 1984.

Terrell, John Upton. Sioux Trail. New York: McGraw-Hill, 1974.

Waldman, Carl. Encyclopedia of North American Tribes. New York: Facts on File, 1988.

Yenne, Bill. Encyclopedia of North American Indian Tribes. New York: Arch Cape Press, a division
of Crown Books, 1986.

Above. A typical Plains Indian village with buffalo meat hanging to dry.

Sioux were brave warriors and used war clubs in battle.

47

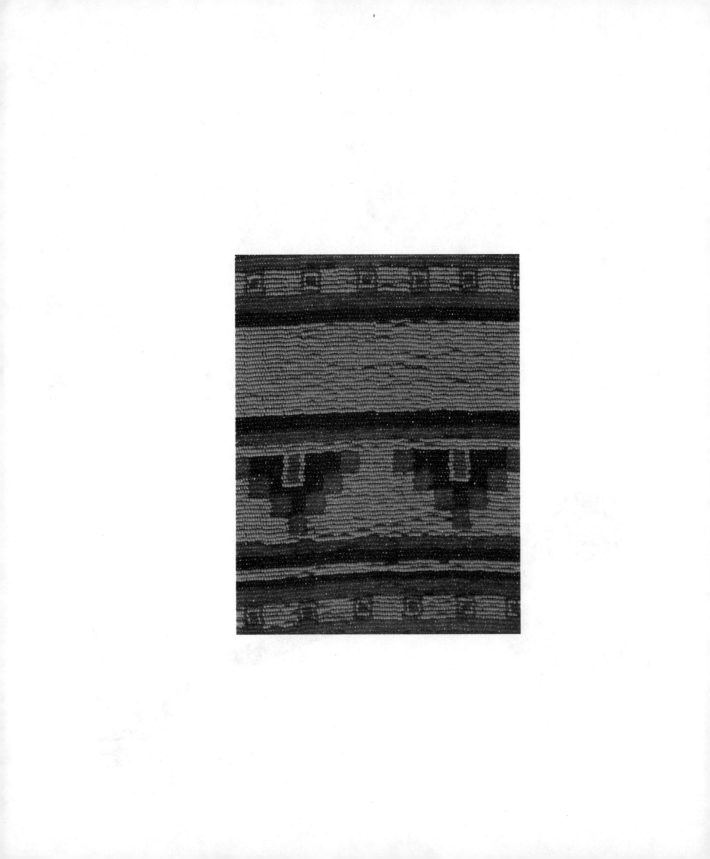